Sunlight Across Your Laugh Lines

Kristen Rae Drake

BookLeaf
Publishing

Presentation by *BookLeaf Publishing*

Web: www.bookleafpub.com

E-mail: info@bookleafpub.com

ISBN: 9789358369137

First edition 2023

DEDICATION

To all the young hearts yearning for love, hoping to belong, and dreaming of peace:

Be wild, free bird.

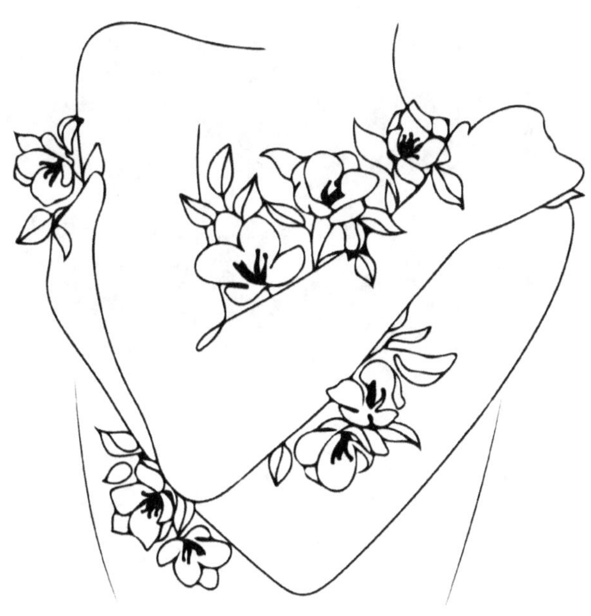

ACKNOWLEDGEMENT

Friends and family, you are so kind and supportive. I cherish your hugs and blessings.

Mom, thank you for your patience, love, and outfits.

Bry, you can do this!

Nick and Kiley, thank you for going to Godspell, being the flower girl & ring bearer, and listening to every version of the national anthem with me.

To my husband, Chase, your smile embodies the warmth of the sun. Thank you for showing me the meaning of unconditional love.

Choo choo!

PREFACE

I grew up near a sugar cane plantation on the island of Oahu, Hawaii. Every morning, my family and I woke up to the sound of a rooster greeting us at dawn, beckoning us to open our sleepy eyes. The burning stalks of sugar cane lingered in the air like the smell of flambéed yams on Christmas morning. I remember the spray of the warm saline ocean against my little feet, and the deep-rooted sense of *ohana* (family) from loved ones and island locals so friendly, I would call them *"Uncle"* or *"Auntie."*

Then my nuclear family was unbound, and I was swept away to Southern California, only a shadow of paradise. I missed the courtship of the ukulele playing island lullabies, and most of all, I longed for my *ohana*.

I scratched my pen onto my notebooks, hoping it would cut through the emptiness I felt inside. Words transformed into poems and songs... and decades later, materialized into self-love and inner peace.

Under the La Jolla Sky

strokes of a cloud's breath
the predecessor of diamonds
Mr. Pelican dives for supper

"It's cold, and I crave your coat,
your arms, your eyelashes."

pause

"Please undo the laces you have around my
heart."

but I brace myself

"Perhaps you needn't go away."

"You mustn't make a broth out of these tears."

"Then stop leading me on," I says.

whilst the tangerine orb
sets completely,
horizonish hues
catch the last blush of cloudlings

dissipates.
what my love does

"Farewell, farewell..."
until morrow you shall be risend
as a fire dove in the high.

The Waiting Hours

the crickets scream until sunlight

The Waiting Hours.

forged in
the conundrum-ical
fantasti-cisms

bellowing out all.
the love.
i salvaged.
for you.

all bets are off.

no longer are you the Knight,
the night you preyed with her longer

knees roughened,
skin glued to pews

i prayed like a howling concubine.

but your sorrow-fuls
and sorrow-ings

moved like molasses
in the moonlight.

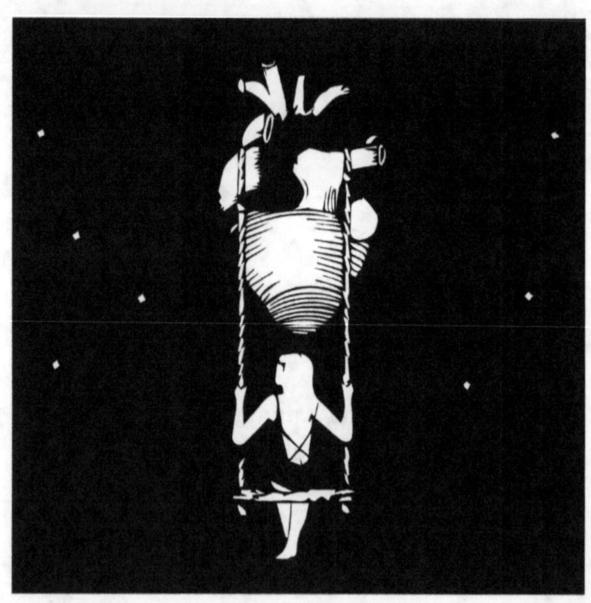

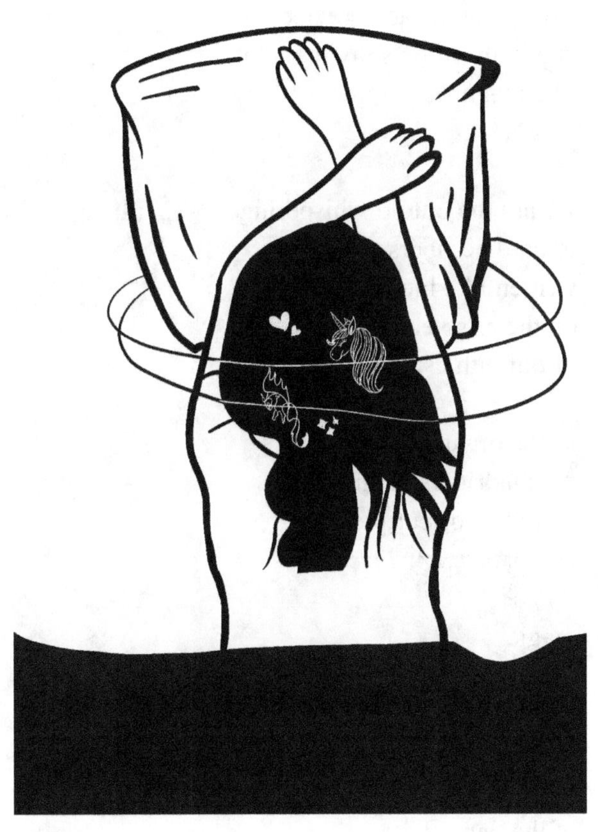

Catacombs

in the catacombs of our asylum
I find you in each crevice
and your pillows invite me in
like magnets
magic

we are the untold whisperings
of cardiac fibers stretching
written like hieroglyphs
on the crisp echoey walls
of our eith

as the organ plays
the madrigals of singsong
melodies of our plea:
come forth, my love

magic
like magnets

I find you there
on each corner
of the damp lairs

in the catacombs of our asylum.

The Lover's Cove

A lover's cove.
'Pon wet sheets
and body heat.

'Tween moans and groans.
Limbs interlaced,
thrusts into the core
with a stallion pace.

A hunger embedded in need
to relieve the fire
with slow brushstrokes
to quench the desire.

Tongue slithers
until stems quiver.
Mouths collide.
The slipping and sliding
satiates the thirst.

With bodies unbinding.

The cove,
that sweet lover's cove.

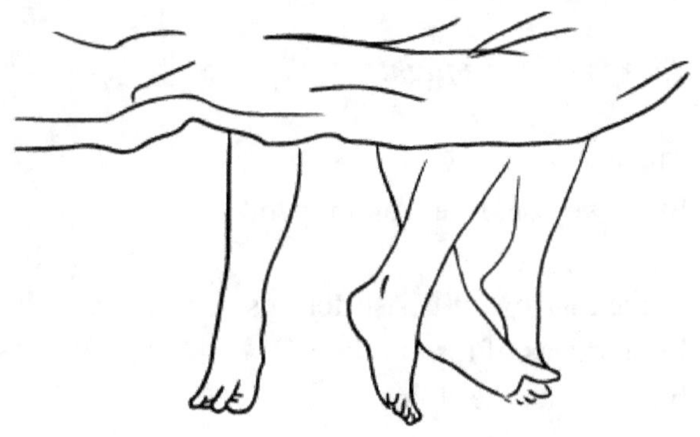

Lioness

The Siren disintegrates
into the fiery mourning sky.
Storm-clouds rage from her eyes.

Parched petals parade down the valley,
shadows of Saturn, lustings, and lace.

Take flight, take flight.

The blaze.
Shall we rise, ripen, and repent?

In the marrow of her sufferings,
lily gardens of torn limbs
birthed from her loins.

The tormentors polish their wide eyes,
inviting the lambs to feast
on the braised humanity in her windows.

Clouded with shrouds of
tainted maiden-cloth,
resurrected in bile and blood-letting,
emerges the Lioness
adorned in stars and marigold.

Letter to Lilyflower

Lilyflower,

don't let a man
have that much
power over you.

"but i so so,
so-so likening"

grateful for the wise domes.
look out for
garden gnome trickeries.

gone gone
done done away.

Petals

Red roses
spilled on
white sheets…

Stained
on glacial
nights.

When she told me
about her
crushed petals,
I believed her.

Why didn't you
Believe?

Dandelion

Dandelion,

Wish, wish

further into the wind

windows closed shut

pursed pillows

wish, wish

breathe life

Be wild, free bird.

Haiku I

sear the sage at dusk

cleanse the recollections of

breathing into you

Moonfall

Meet me
by moonfall
like we used to.
Steal away
for a moment
with me.

Your rib
bestowed
to another.
She, the Tail.

So lovely.
Her heart
so pure,
your
Beloved.

But meet me
under moonfall.
No need
for our
fingertips
to touch.

Just breathe,
one last,
with me.

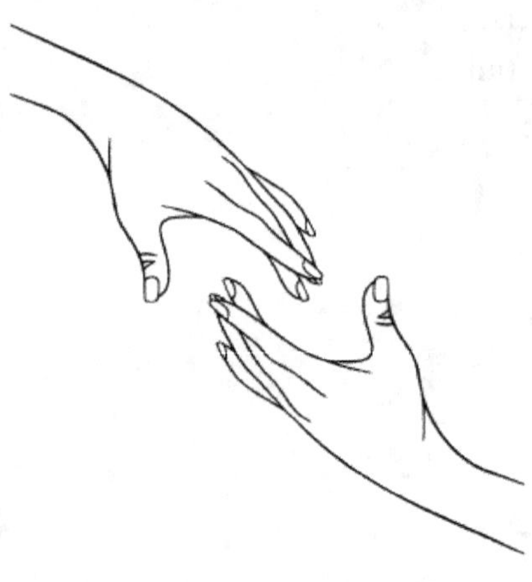

Surfboard

I'll marry you
only if…
Only if
you lose
fifty pounds.

The weight
of those conditions
crushed me
more
in that moment
than when
I was told

I was too fat
to get onto
a surfboard.

I never learned.

If I'm too fat
to marry,
please let go
of my
love handles.

They don't
belong to
you.

Friend

Would I invite her back in?
Welcome my old friend,

 Loneliness.

So words could flow
like rivers once again?

Is Sorrow
    the only
welcomer of words?

Not Joy
        who quells the ache,
        and brings Grief to an
                                end?

Diaphragmatic quakes.
Laugh lines
to smother the Anguish.

Like two roads,
we bend.
Let her go now,
as we transcend.

Goodbye, Loneliness,

Laughter is my new
friend.

Mr. Toucan

Dear Mr. Toucan,

Went to Woolworths the other day
and saw your old roommate's mug
on a cereal box--
reminded me to
return your measuring cup,
reminded me to look you up,
so I can show you
a picture of
my newborn pup.

She's cute,
you know,
she has my eyes,
she gets tipsy
off of Kahlua pie.

Mr. Toucan,

I'll write you back
when I'm done
driving.

Dear Mr. Toucan,

What do you do
when your beak
becomes dull from
kissing the Mrs.
atop
the canopy layer?

Dear Mr. Toucan,

I found a hair
in my soup
the other day…

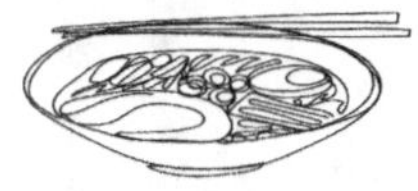

Dear Mr. Toucan,

Read a poem written
by an anonymous bloke
thought I'd share a story
about how he choked.
Once Upon A Time…

Dear Mr. Toucan,

Please respond!
Your reticence caused me
to devour a cookie jar
full of
Diddlydoodlidees!

2 Days Later…

Dear Mr. Toucan,

Why so quiet?
You think I smell
like spoiled milk!?
Go sulk over a
bowl of
Fruitily Loopins;
I'm through with you!

Pizza

I spent years
chasing after
the kind of body
that would
make my mom
happy.

Now I strut
my jiggly stuff.

I work out
because
I like to move
to Reggaeton,
Trap,
& EDM.

My stems lean,
arms toned.

But my abs
will always show
my love
for
pizza.

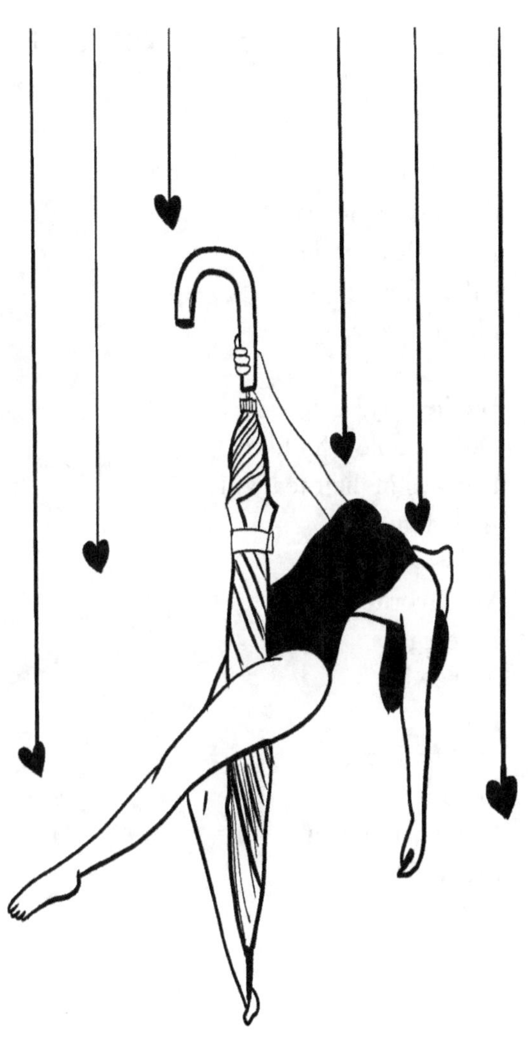

Jasmine Green Tea

May I order
the mushy globes
in plastic aquariums,
half sweet,
please?

By the way,
Only people who like
Bubbles in their tea will
Ascertain…

My favorite
beverage
is chewier
than a
fruity rolli*o, o, o.*

Don't care about
the weight
I gain.

Grocery List

Yes, get the eggs and
only if you like to shop in the rain, bring your
umbrella.

And
remember to nourish yourself
even when you want to

Eat everything and
nothing with arugula
or radishes. I completely
understand if you
go away for the weekend to
have paella by the sea.

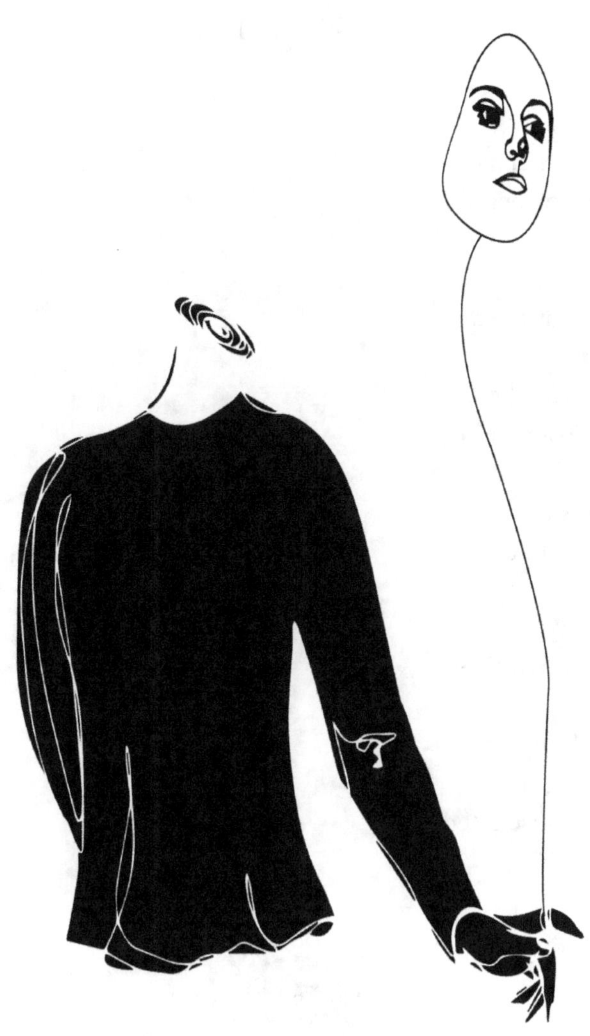

Beacon

A menagerie of
melancholia.

A fading
marionette.

And then.
Your smile.

A beacon
of light
across
my
frown lines.

Your kiss on
night two
resuscitated me.

Eyelash

I love it when you
get an eyelash
stuck in your eye.
I know it tickles,
forces you to pause,
let down your disguise.

So lost in thought
for hours.
How can I
disrupt such
concentration.
What's on your mind?

You say
you don't like ice cream.
"It's the texture."
That just means I have another
few spoonfuls to taste
the sweet morsels.
I love the sugar high.

It reminds me of
how I felt
when we first met.
You said "Hi there!"

"How's it going?"
Instant companions.
I'm still addicted to
your smile.

Now you sleep
so soundly next
to me.
Sometimes I
pinch myself.
I can't believe
you're forever mine.

Your eyelashes,
your mouth,
your breath.
Your "hello"s
and "hi there"s.
"I love you"s.
I will treasure
for life.

Little Spoon

I promise
to try
not to tell
the whole world
you're the
little spoon.

The one who
fits so nicely
against my
sourdough form.

How did I
get so lucky
to be the one
to enjoy the
symphony of
your gentle snores?

Little Spoon,
let's stay in bed.
Your warm
layer fits
so snugly
against mine.

Haiku II

let me be the rays

sunlight across your laugh lines

until my last dawn

Little Feet

I dream of
little feet
little toes.
Let's help
them grow
into
the best
versions of
you and me.

You, strong
and intelligent.
Confident.
Me, nurturing
and soft.
Peaceful.
Us, loving
and creative.

Little feet
to fill
big shoes.
Can't wait
to see
them grow.

Strong
and intelligent.
Confident.
Nurturing
and soft.
Peaceful.
Loving
and creative.

Little feet to
march forth
with you and me.